Finding the Islands

W.S. Merwin

North Point Press
San Francisco · 1982

Some of the poems in part one of this collection were
first published in a limited edition by The Windhover
Press in 1978.

Printed in the United States of America
Library of Congress Catalogue Card Number:
82-081481
ISBN: 0-86547-088-x (cloth) / 0-86547-089-8 (paper)

For Robert and Anne Aitken

Contents

I   Feathers from the Hill

Time of Tree Cutting

Cold August
mice roll
empty nutshells

—

Darkness that covers
and uncovers the moon
shadow of a wing

—

Waking
hanging upward into the rushing summer
calling

—

Everything is
the answer
too fast

—

Where the cliff
splits
later the dove nests

—

Stony slopes buckwheat smell
wings of landing plover
shiver

—

Nearby one monkey at sunset
ate in silence
watching the lightning

—

The colors look back at the trees
but the birds shut their eyes
thinking to see it all again

—

Along the white hill
owl floats
weighed down with moonlight

—

Nobody knows who lived here
the roof is gone
the eastern cloud swallows the stars

—

Sunlit woods
feather falls
everywhere ready for it

—

Laughter of crows late in the month
spun saucer settling
sunset moving south

Summer Canyon

Some of the mayflies
drift on into June
without their names

—

Spring reappears in the evening
oyster cloud sky catches in pines
water light wells out of needles after sundown

—

On small summit pine hollow
field chickweed under trees
split white petals drifting over shadow

—

Two crows call to each other
flying over
same places

—

In high mountains
the late grass
grows as fast as it can

—

Because of things not even remembered
we are here
listening to the water

—

Three broad blue petals
I do not know
what kind of flower

—

Among the pines above me
flowers from days ago
are about to open

—

Leaves never seen before
look how they have grown
since we came here

—

After midnight wind drops
belled cat walks the hillside
under black trees

—

Day's end green summer stillness
pine shadows drift far out
on long boards

—

Mourning dove sound
cricket sound
no third

—

Afternoon breeze prowls
with a tail
through tall green upland grass

—

Half moon light midsummer
unseen pheasant among bright rocks
echoes its own voice

———

All day the wind blows
and the rock
keeps its place

———

A silence begins
soon many feet
are heard running

———

Black tree trunks in shade
outside a house
with wooden floors

———

Birds on the roof
if I went up to see
they would be gone

———

For each voiceless flower
there is a voice among
the absent flowers

———

Far away a dog barks
on a windy hilltop
beyond which the sun is setting

———

Sunlight after rain
reflections of ruffled water
cross the ceiling

———

High in the east full moon
and far below on the plain
low clouds and lightning

—

Birds hidden
in moonlit boughs
call from dreams

—

Hot wind at noon
pine cones from dying tree
fall full of seeds

—

Early dusk
pine needles already shining
before rain

—

Line of smoke
writes on
sunlight

—

Flecks of bright down
sail up the day
clear out of the canyon

—

Mountain of
butterflies
hurries

—

Whistle of
mourning dove's wings
stretches the shadows

—

Early I saw
where the sun comes from
here

—

Under a pine at noon
I listen to plates
clattering in a kitchen

—

At the same time every day
clouds come over the mountain
what was I thinking when they appeared

—

Jay clatters through dark pines
it remembers
something it wants there among them

—

Tree toads tighten their notes
numberless yellow daisies
rise through gray grass

—

Sudden rain
army of light passes
with dark footprints

—

Lizard grows up
to be gray twig
in summer

—

Opening my eyes I see
burning alone in blue
the morning star

—

Solitary wasp writes
white eggs
up south window

———

Thistledown
already far from its flower
and still snow on the peaks

———

Young deer standing in headlights
in ditch below cliff
cars coming both ways

———

South slope running to seed
chipmunk squeak shadows
crickets trill long dry grass

———

Even among spoons
favorites emerge
days rising through water

———

Gray voice
nuthatch after sunset
nothing to call it

———

No earlier
could anything that is here
have been

———

A thistledown
is the moon for a moment
then thistledown again

———

Lizard rainwalk on bright boards
rain stops and looks out
washed air

—

Moth studies bark
not moving while
daylight lasts

—

For an age lizards run on gray places
and grown beetles set out from pines
in the heat

—

Too late the chain saws
scream into echoing trunks
finding corridors empty

—

Gray rocks darken
wet bronze pine bark echoes jay shriek
across tall rainy yellow grass

—

Jay calls at night and wakes
flying through dark branches
faster than it can see

—

Pine needles many as stars
one word for all the trees ever seen
and their lifetimes

—

Yellow clothesline empty
raw pole in woods
rain drips from clothespins

—

One night for a moment
beautiful animal
never seen before
—

With lengthening summer
the wild dove's flight
grows louder
—

Steep yellow grass rain
transparent everything I remember
other lives
—

August midnight
horse snorts
in cricket dark
—

Garbage dog bell cat
kitchen mouse banister jay
ceiling chipmunk
—

Afternoon sun wet boughs
smell of autumn in August
schoolbell anvil echoes in empty woods
—

Pines against sky of mist
where I am now
in a breath of a mountain
—

Night of rain onto late summer
cool morning again
cloud canyon

Sound of Rapids of Laramie River in Late August

White flowers among white stones
under white windy aspens
after night of moonlight and thoughts of snow

Fireweed

One morning the days have grown shorter
and fireweed is purple
on the mountains
—

Yellow-winged
grasshoppers clatter through high
windy valley
—

Sound of rain on tent
light from wet sagebrush
on all sides
—

Sundown across shallow stream
magpies bathe together
in aspen thicket
—

After rain cold evening
gray clouds dark south gorge
smell of more rain coming
—

Horses and trees move
in same waves cool night
summer really gone

—

Breasts of swallows turning
flash in morning
among their voices

—

Meadow of sagebrush in flower
cat sits in the middle
fur of morning sunlight

—

Sound of tires on cobbles
decades ago
roars past me now with no car

—

Afternoon moves through
empty tent
cushion at foot of pole

—

Human shadows
walk on tent wall
inside and outside

—

Old woman young woman
baby in green knapsack shouting
past tree after tree

—

Afternoon breeze comes down valley
following small stream
and finds horses

—

Knothole looks out
through a branch
that has come and gone

—

Flies convene
in a patch of sunlight
a day on a calendar

—

Same gong
each hand strikes
different note

—

I leave the tent breathing
without dreams
and walk out on my own

—

Child holds hourglass
above his head
and looks up

—

Last day of August
western bluebirds in
pine shadow

—

In full day
tent pole passes through
big star

—

A moment at a time
the mountain rises
out of empty sky

In the Red Mountains

Blue chairs hang empty
waiting in clear
September sky
—

Daybreak mist in valley
skylark rises
through green floor of cloud
—

Light evening rain
eleven magpies
dance in twilight
—

Yellow light
memory in aspens
of first frost
—

Chainsaw three minutes
hours later in rain
smell of resin
—

Wrinkled mountains
end of autumn day
peach down

—

The colors move
but not
the evening clouds

—

Moth shadow circles floor
moth alights
by my foot

—

Through black pines
colors on the mountain
climb down the days

—

On summits last year's snow
gray with waiting
clear sky white clouds of autumn

—

Slow bee
still searching yellow day
before frost

—

Leaves begin to fall
old road appears on the mountains
never anyone's

—

Hawk flake turns
slowly above ridges
in far blue eye

—

Aspen glare
migrant blackbirds'
reed-voices
—

Gold trees
turn into
smoke again
—

At last
leaves fall
from bare sky
—

Leaves still on branches
turn at night into
first snow
—

Many times clouds were mountains
then one morning mountains
woke as clouds
—

Feet in mist
feel the earth move
from under
—

After sunrise
autumn mists part
showing another valley
—

Two snows come and gone
brown cows' valley pastures
gray undersides of olive leaves
—

I see my parents
through a grove of white trees
on a day of winter sunlight

—

Shadow ravine
snow blue as smoke full of sunlight
over black fire

—

Wakes of light
ray out on dark pond
where ducks swim before winter

—

Snow blows from the roof
the whole room
flies out over the white valley

Road

In early snow
going to see a friend
I pass thousands of miles of fences

Island City

Green corn stalks rustle
beginning to dry
on a hill above the sea

—

Pile of box houses
with wires on every side
and box voices and box dogs

—

Around a corner
somebody who's a city
pounds all day on a tin door

—

Only two houses away
a neighbor
is a piano playing

—

A breeze through the house
and one fly rushes
from window to window

—

Morning noon and evening
the old woman turns on the sprinkler
and watches

—

The landlord's children
lock up their dog
and shout at it

—

Living it up
in the afternoon
at the shopping center

—

Under the traffic light
silent paper boy
watches the cars

—

Whole crowd nosing
for shade for the baby
while they go fishing

—

Backs in a row at the sea's edge
bow late in the day
hooking tiny fish

—

Little girl's belly
old man's belly
a sail on the horizon

—

Old dog under a bush
head on his paws
watches waves climb the sand

—

All the guests in the neighbor's garden
ask where the neighbors will go
now he's retiring

—

Toward the sea
wings of flies flash
with sunset

—

Suddenly wrinkles appear
on the water
and then are gone again

—

Going away over water
a cloud
from a cloud

—

So many lives in the evening
staring at the one
program

—

When his television
is off
the neighbor can't stop coughing

—

As I grow older
the cities spread
over the earth

—

A tree stirs
and the curtain
draws back from the window

—

Ward of unlit terraces
the hour of night barks
and echoes

—

At night the autumn mist
arrives and arrives in silence
but the eaves drip through the dark

—

Sound of late tires carries
from an unseen street
through cool leaves

—

It isn't the moon
but the city reflected
from the house fronts on the hill

—

One cricket starts up
in the still moonlight
and wakes the refrigerator

—

Rain from the full moon
all at once washes away
deep dust

—

By the setting moon
a rat runs
on the dry leaves of the woodrose

—

Sleeping I saw the new moon
through the open window
of an unknown kitchen

—

Lizard clacks at daybreak
in the dark of mango trees
when the morning star is alone
——
Packing again
to the sound
of autumn rain

By the Mango Trees

A little higher
the green hill hides
in rain

———

The trees bow with the wind
but the houses
forget

———

Rain on the tin roof
lizard hands on the tin ceiling
listening

———

In the evening sunlight
the hill pasture
is ripening

———

Lizard just hatched
such a hurry
tail gets in front of the head

———

A spider hangs
from a new thread
in the light from the window

—

Lizard runs out on a beam
shits and
looks down

—

White balsam flowers
moons in
full moonlight

—

Late at night
the dogs bark for hours
then the rain comes

—

Great dipper stands
on its handle
leaning against the paling sky

—

When the rooster crows
a rat shakes
the orange tree

—

Old dry banana leaf
one of my aunts
but I can't remember which

—

Loud yellow truck passes
the yellow lilies
in the wind

—

Living at the farm
she airs her baby
up and down the road
—

How time disappears
while we live under
the big tree

Warm Pastures

Half the night sky deep cloud
and rain falls
through moonlight
—

Moonlight before dawn
voices of plovers waking in flight
over foggy pastures
—

Birds' feet
scratch the tin roof
daybreak
—

Lighthouse goes on
flashing flashing
as the sun rises
—

Still not seasoned
rooftree runs through row
of old sparrow nests
—

The first light
is climbing the road
through black trees

—

Hearing rain on big leaves
I look up
and all the white birds have gone

—

Can't see the rain
but see where
the sand jumps

—

Loud rain
fog on the hills
mud from the faucets

—

Week of rain
voice of ground dove
from wet woods

—

As he mends
the wire pasture fence
the waves keep breaking behind him

—

Black cows
by late morning
are the big tree's shadow

—

How far the plover comes
to stand in the grass
by the stairs

—

Peel the round-ended
pineapple fields
off the raw hills

—

Crop-duster pilot goes
home and washes his
hands his hands

—

Christmas Eve bright sunlight
white smoke
smelling of sugar

—

Sun drops into smoke
the cane fields appear
burning

—

In the wild
they know
they are rare

—

In the gold evening
the tall trees are leaning
toward the flying voices

—

Shadow
overflows a spring
down in the pasture

—

Another cloud
at evening passing
the distant island

—

Suddenly the shadows
of the wheeling plovers
go out

—

As the year was ending
I heard a breath
start the tin windmill

—

When the moon sets
the sea slowly
disappears

—

Fond of the clock
because of the hours
it has told

—

In the night grass
cricket is travelling
into one note

—

I wake touching her
and lie still to listen
to the warm night

Sheep Clouds

Wake on the train
and they tell you
what you didn't see

—

In the mist at daybreak
row of socks hanging
over the vegetable garden

—

Once you leave
you have a name
you can't remember

—

Already at the thought
of the late spring
the window is open

—

Mist fades in the sun
sheep lean into the wall
shirt breathes at a window

—

In the spring evening
a crow calls
and I come back from the years

—

The cornflowers
keep painting
the faded air

—

Long twilight
before midsummer
all the clouds are moon

—

Old branch alive alive
moored in the darkening sky
sound of the stream

—

The moth brings
the map
of both sides

—

Just before dawn
the nightingale
starts something new

—

Midsummer stars fade
the oriole echoes
the nightingale

—

When it says
goodbye
say thank you

—

Deep in cloud
a day with summer flowers
and small bells ringing
———

Starts too near
ever to
arrive
———

Late in summer
the birds draw
closer together
———

In a summer of mist
through the evening
a road of mist
———

Hay in and a cow sick
the unwatched television
flickers on his face
———

What is an itch
that nobody should speak
well of it
———

Sun sinks on red pastures
and a dog barks
at the sound of a closing door
———

Oh the sun sets in the oaks
and the white lady
calls to the mice of the fields
———

Stars of August what
are you
doing

—

Moon setting
in the oak tree
wakes one blackbird

—

Bright September
the shadow of the old walnut tree
has no age

—

On the reflections of the freight cars
after the frost
water lilies

II   Turning to You

To Dana with the Gift of a Calendar

In the winter in the first month of every
year of my life I was
looking for you
—

when your eyes open
I fall toward you
out of myself
—

when I am away from you uncounted
clouds of fish are calling in the seas
and nobody hears them
—

we are waiting
to be picked up by
the same wind
—

we go to the mountain together
and we find a house
high in the pines
—

we lie on the floor in each other's arms
and listen to the drums
and the wolves

—

you leave your sunglasses on the south sea wall
near the print of our bodies
in the evening sand

—

we go up to a cold high lake
and make love
before dark

—

we lie naked by the tower at night
hearing the sheep chewing
in the moonlight by the wall

—

we are attacked
and we
are one

—

the soft rain
for seven years I have felt your skin
and the light of your fingers

—

as the year turns
in the night
may we wake to each other

Turning to You

Seeing my shadow on the cloud
I have reached for your hand
and found it
—

There was never a time
when you were not walking toward me
from under great trees
—

Driving up the mountain
the first evening
watching you
—

The fish swim by our feet
as we eat from the same hand
and drink from the same mouth
—

The leaves are talking in the sky
we fly among them playing
below us the ages of our green star
—

From the rock pool I see you
sitting on your heels watching me
long thigh of late sunlight eyes still

—

As we move together on your old bed
they are lighting fuses
for the new year

—

Tea in bed in the mountains
all morning watching the snow fall
in May

—

Autumn dusk in an empty
quarry town paved with marble
I feel the warmth of your body

—

All day together
in town out of town
how sharp the tops of the green mountains

—

Late I came
to the joy of this
whatever I have is yours

—

After seven years
still we feed each other like birds
by the breaking waves

—

Yours is the radiance
you say is mine since you met me
pearl of heaven

—

I travel on and on
until there is only you
my homeland and morning

—

I want to be buried
under your heart
where I was born

Living Together

I have not forgotten
the first touch of your fingers
I listen to the stream in the night

—

Last night as we left
the moon rose
like a house burning in a cloud

—

Meeting we stood on a small bridge
with the world
flowing under us

—

Once there were many days and nights
and then there was
only yours

—

When we kissed
all the leaves of the warm
spring forest gathered us

—

Afterwards we came
to the same words
in the same voice

—

Why have you
hidden from me
why have I ever hidden from you

—

The moon is late and there is no wind
soft breath in the darkness
I try to see you

—

In the dark I think of you
naked in my arms in the sun
on the porch by the pines

—

In the sound of your breath
I feel the tips of your fingers
your thighs and the tight moist hair

—

When I think of your skin
the pearl shines
in the light that never changes

—

I hold in my eyes
the pink cloth stretching
as you walked on the sea wall

—

I like to walk behind you
to watch and remember
and look forward

—

My eye rests
above your hip where the smooth
rise slopes inward
———

When I hear the rain in the leaves
long before morning
I move to you
———

When we open our eyes
to each other
it is morning
———

No one will ever see you
as you appeared
when we woke
———

In the sunny forest
we lie on the grass
hearing the sea
———

Each of us
as a child
watched a mountain
———

Every day we look at each other
and at the sea
and at the mountain
———

We two swam naked
in the clear bay talking and laughing
at noon
———

I remember lines I have read
lying on the shore
with my hand on you

—

We stand in the daylight
letting the same water
run on us both

—

We took off
across the country
as we said we would

—

Candles in paper bags
on a white wall
appear to us both at once

—

We stood in a garden by a wall
and the evening star
took us by surprise

—

Not having dressed
we watched the lights go on
out on the plain beyond the valley

—

And we let the telephone
go on ringing
and ringing

—

In a cold
summer you heard
the nightingale

—

In the snow your cold face
presses against mine
laughing as you hold me

—

In the winter
under your jacket
how hot the sides of your breasts are

—

Whatever they said
we would not dance
with anyone else

—

We stand in line
taking up
one space

—

How many times
we have eaten
touching

—

When it flooded we curled up
on the one dry spot
and that was our bed

—

We watch the lizard's feet
on the tin ceiling
drumming with rain

—

We live where plovers
fly past our bed calling
through the winter nights

—

We call each other to see
the rainbow the sun on the mountain
the coast under the moon
——

We talk while the sunlight
moves across the bed
what are we saying
——

We tell each other of a language
and it breathes
between us
——

You say that our
minds are one
and alone in the world
——

In my dreams we keep
travelling together
face to face
——

When we get home
from wherever it is
we take off our clothes
——

Nobody in the world
knows how you
smell to me
——

I hold your toes and your ankles
kiss the backs of your knees
draw them apart
——

Through the hours of the day
I carry in my mouth
the taste of you

———

My tongue follows
the smooth sides
of each of your folds

———

After watching them
all the way home
I feel your legs around me

———

You rise to me
like the waves between the rocks
calling me

———

The veins on your eyelids swell
and your eyelids
and your wide eyes

———

From the way
I say your name
I always know

Long Love

By now whatever
I see is lovely
seems a reflection of you
—

Before day I lie watching
your face asleep
on the same pillow
—

Our breath has mingled
for so many years
it moves as one
—

From long love
I look at you
from long love I see you
—

Again and again
with you lying beside me
I have needed nothing
—

Together with you
I do not miss
even the first nights and days
—
How could I
have known of wanting
you after years

The Mountains

Our names surrounded
by a heart
entwine in the dark

—

When we are apart I can
smell you on me
even from far away

—

I believed that after
the last tree fell
you would still be there

—

Even after the lightning
and the waking
there would be you

—

I believed that after the final
rain I would still
be able to feel you

—

Star space
and the unthinkable cold
but you there
——
I saw the mountains
where we were going
where you would be

On the Mountain

Across the mountain I see you
across the crater
we live on
—

you avoid the words
about you
like a mountain goat
—

today I saw your face in a pool on the mountain
for a long time beside mine
looking up from the sky
—

leaves of the acacias
in the warm rain
your fingers in the day
—

you are walking in the trees on the ridge
when the trades are
waving them
—

long ago it was raining and we stepped
over the burned mountain stones
and kissed in a cloud
—

today on the mountain you turn
you raise your hand you call
you start toward me

Hours

Now I can
see you
at all times
—

in the first light of morning
you turning to me
smiling with the whole of your dark body
—

loving with our mouths
and making love
in the gold afternoon sunlight
—

at night with streetlight in the room
hearing you call out to me
above the rumble of the subway
—

late in the morning
the rain going on falling and we
never wanting to get up
—

just as the sun is going down
so that we have
supper late in bathrobes
——

standing together in the still house
when the guests have gone home at last
stirring the sweetness between us
——

waking together
in the middle of the night
by surprise
——

the hours of you are without
number and each
has no end
——

do I love you more when it is raining
more in summer or winter
turned one way or the other
——

do I love you more when you are too
hot in bed
or when we are cool after the shower
——

all the time I love
most your own longing
drawing me

Green Island

The same sunlight on the wet
banana leaves by the window
and on your wet skin
—

I want you to be
the air in the house
the footfall inside me
—

Through our love the beacon
goes on turning
and the sea glides in
—

I want to be the dream
you feel
and the light you wake to
—

The rain gives way to clear
night and you draw
me to you in the cool daybreak

I want you to be
the smell of the bed
and the fingers of the day

—

You began our love
with flowers I
had never heard of

—

I want to be
the leaves moving
day and night in your valley

—

When I look at your dark hair
it seems enough
all by itself

—

I want you to be
the moon again
in the still mango trees

—

In your voice the rain
is finding its way to the stream
above the sea

At Home

As the ants know
where the honey is
I know the way to you
—

where we live
we look far out to sea
and our clothes are behind us in the bedroom
—

here on a shirt is a scar
of your round stitches
pulling apart again
—

we saved some of the old calendars
for their beauty
I look at the numbers
—

one year on your birthday
after years together
we planted that big tree
—

we remember each other
as we will never
be again
—
I think of you with nothing on
leaning across the sink
looking into the mirror
—
I find you cooking
in your torn
underpants worn low
—
each time you
set the table
it is a world never repeated
—
you read lying on the mattress
wearing nothing
but your glasses
—
sometimes it is true
we do not go out enough
we stay home

February in the Valley

It is winter still
but this morning while
we made love the rose opened

—

as we enter
the tender rapids
you look up and tell me you dreamed this

Dark Side

If I were to talk of you
how would anyone know
what the words meant
—

you walk on a black road
brown water running beside you
eyes staring and the night coming with dark clouds
—

you smile standing
in the green waves in the sunlight
with your hands in your dark wet hair
—

some of what you
say to me I forget
but I remember you saying it in the dark
—

always I want
you to say
more
—

I see the back
of the mirror
you hold up to the light

—

I watch you open
your eyes wider and wider
into the mirror

—

you stand beside me
when we have just
dried each other

—

you breathe above my ear
you call out to me
from that close

—

I hear your bare step on the bare floor
when I hold your dark
feet in my hands

—

the earth is bleeding into the sea far out
we look away
one side of the heart is dark

Winter Storm

In February lightning at night
wind and rain from the south and west
fell fruit trees in the fenced garden
—

in the cloudy morning we lie reading together
the hand you give me
is the hand you gave me
—

we were together first in February
at night on a mountain and the wind
blew the rain
—

where we lay we heard the drops
in the night-green leaves
and saw the white flowers nodding
—

now when you are in another room
I think of what you feel like
when we are in the same room
—

after breakfast
when you climb on me
I help you up

—

I want to remember clearly
from the beginning
come and greet me

—

you are made of petals and leaves
on which the rain
at night has been falling

—

each of us is one
side of the rain
we have only one shadow

—

how can we forget
anything at which
we have both been present

—

we are what we waited for all the dry time
the valley sighing
water trickling through the grass

St. Valentine's Eve

I watched the late sunlight
on the green valley above the sea
where we came to live

—

in the young year
again I am thankful
for your small breasts

—

after the rains the days are longer
at dusk a bell frog follows the swollen stream
down to the watercress meadow

—

hearing you in the house
I think of the ways
you put yourself around me

—

the night is so still
gecko cricket and an unknown voice
we do not know our age

—

I remember you talking
to me a long time in whispers
our early nights our late mornings
—
you can do it all with your eyes
you can do it all
with any motion

Design by David Bullen
Typeset in Mergenthaler Bembo
by Wilsted & Taylor
Printed by Thomson-Shore
on acid-free paper